The Storyteller's Return

The Storyteller's Return

STORY POEMS

Opal Palmer Adisa

IAN RANDLE PUBLISHERS
Kingston • Miami

First published in Jamaica, 2022 by
Ian Randle Publishers
16 Herb McKenley Drive
Box 686
Kingston 6
www.ianrandlepublishers.com

ISBN 978-976-8286-46-8

National Library of Jamaica Cataloguing-in-Publication Data

Name: Adisa, Opal Palmer, author.

Title: The storyteller's return: poetic stories / Opal Palmer Adisa.

Description: Kingston : Ian Randle Publishers, 2022.

Identifier: ISBN 978-976-8286-46-8 (pbk)

Subjects: LCSH : Poetry – Black authors | Jamaican poetry

Classification: DDC 811 - - dc 23

Cover Illustration by Kokab Zohoori-Dossa
Book Design by Ian Randle Publishers

Printed and Bound in the United States of America

this collection is dedicated to

those who have returned,

those who want to return,

those who can't return, and

those whose return is spiritual...

Contents

part i

home is a stolen
memory
locked away
in a forgotten
time

rubicon

at fifteen she got on a plane and left

if you leave you'll never be able to return

at twenty she got on a plane and returned

if you return you will not remember
that you can never leave

at thirty she forgot what she knew and left again

if returning was to happen
she would have to sing a sankofa dirge

at fifty she returned   heedless
of the smell of longing

home was tattooed on her brain
a brand without a house

my grandmother has been locked in a
house made of wood
with barred windows
so night is perpetual
her nails scrape the wall and a tiny voice
that does not belong to her squeals *you
can never remove
me from home*

cleromancy

whenever she swam in the ocean
bones scraped her feet

tugged at her arms   pulled her down to be with them

you're the only one who can tell our stories

they bobbed around her   bulky bones out of place in the sea bed

see we are alive   alive

gills growing from their knuckles
their breaths vaporous

she collected these sea-laden bones

set them down with reverence on her veranda
every day she passed them
they pointed out something new

we are returning

they hummed all through the night
transecting her dreams

we are making our way   back home

my grandma has been dreaming me
telling me to *come home*
i'm home   i assert
this is a house not a home she snaps
go home where the night seeks you
to bend its power

home

flesh seared as love

smoke rising in the blue hills in the morning

a bullfrog leaping onto the veranda
then hiding in a flowerpot

a blank slate smudged

home was not all together clean

when grandma had her own
home she left the walls
concrete grey   allowed
devil's ivy to trail from roof
to ground

home again

the first night home   the loudness
of the crickets surprised her
so much was happening outside
that she could not see   when she finally
fell asleep   the stars' winking outside the
uncurtained window cushioned her sleep

after she woke the first morning home   she ran outside
wanting to see if it was real or a memory
the grass was indeed wet with dew that tickled her soles
but it was the beauty of the mountains   verdant and blue
it was the bougainvillea their orange   purple   white   red blossoms
lining and draping the land in unapologetic fierceness
it was the intense and familiar talk of the people   whose speech she understood
words as proverbial as the spittle in her mouth
she rejoiced   her heart playing a mixed-up tune
her spirit saying thank you for bringing me home

> grandma puts the basin of water to
> warm in the morning sun
> *is only because yu just return*
> she clicks her tongue
> *yu haffi acclimate to home*

crossword

emoh spelt backwards

h

      o

            m

                e   a diagonal landscape

m h   meaning beaten out

oe   love rubbed in

hmfooamtter   a puzzle mother/father
pieces missing

a bed that is clean

a glass of milk

a yard with a tricycle   one wheel missing

a bombay mango tree with a swing affixed
to one of its branches

a wasp nest of expectations

a space to curl up and sleep

you'll always be welcomed

come on home

until yu have yu own home yu *can neva*
be yuself   grandma pauses
her hands are elbow deep in the basin
suds froth the top
her hands make squish-squish music
with the clothes
her fingers are stained blue from the
bluing *so not a duppy can enter*
yu home

memories lie

home is a lie
emotion subvert everything
historians are trustworthy

home smells like a freshly cut lime
seeds dug out before being squeezed into
the glass   pulp clinging to the lid

home is a dresser drawer pulled open
rummage through and under tissue paper and nylon slips
are letters wrapped in a handkerchief

the cursive lean and slanted words are smeared   grandma insists that i listen
I did not mean to…   *home is a fish bowl* she laughs
                                                         falling off the chair   her tears
what's legible is a mystery   water the plants
it was such a long time
whole lines faded   water mark trails
your father was a man sealed into a buried home

glimpse

small feet dash through the living room
run unto the veranda   down the steps
across the path to the front gate
to kiss mommy first

bathed and in a clean dress   you sit for dinner
use your knife and fork   *elbows off the table*

                    is suh home tan grandma bellows turning her
the manners of home are a ritual   back on me but glancing over her shoulder to see
intended to make you a lady   if i'm still listening   *same way suh home tan*
                          she rotates on the chair
see the kite tangled in the cotton tree   toes pointed like a dancer
                          grandma has macramè me
even as you try to run from the dye   a home sweet home
your dress is sullied   a blemish on home

bar the doors

once the storyteller enters

home becomes a public site
a place where logic and love collide

things you have always thought were true
are trapped on the barbed wire as you attempt to escape
the man chasing you for stealing his fruits

my sister and i ran to the door

but daddy had already left

hickory dickory dock   home was under water

home is not located
in a nursery rhyme

grandma kisses her teeth *is not only anansi*
have story fi tell
she gets up with the broom and sweeps the
corners of the ceiling then resits
props her chin in her open palms
clears her throat:
anansi get him story from him mama's titty

accident

Opal Palmer Adisa

when you fall and scrape your knee or elbow
there's no alphabet to shelter home

you remember the night
you   your sister   and mother were
picking your way through a foreign road
to reach a house that would become   home

your mother had gnashed her knee
blood streamed down her leg   grandma ran away from her father's home
pooled at her feet   built herself a round house
                                    planted crotons and put up a triangular sign which
the heavy suitcases made the path zig-zagged   reads
so home seemed that much farther

                                                        dis is fi me home

this is the way you draw a house

2 parallel vertical lines
attached to 2 parallel horizontal lines

add a triangle at the top then 2 square windows
1 rectangular door

my house was ready
tucked at the back of the sugar estate
near the defunct cane factory and the barracks
where the white overseer sometimes visited
in the shadow of night to be with his lover   the maid

frilly curtains transformed my house into a home
shutting out eyes eager for gossip

when i turn on my left side
grandma whispers in my ear
fi keep yu home safe
always enter the front door backwards
i toss in my sleep
If yu waan maintain a home
weh niceness is plenty-plenty
no friend yu close neighbours

how to make a house a home

use a ladder and climb to the roof
if you're afraid of heights   conquer your fear
see what the house sees   notice what blocks
the house's view   listen to the house's grumble
then come down and wash around the house

inside   press your palms to the walls
invite your ancestors   only those who loved
and affirmed you   to smoke out
the house   take a shower
then press your wet body to the walls
so your scent is penetrated
tell the house it is becoming your home
– you might have to really convince it
the house will transform when and only
when you kneel to your own desires
and rinse home in the ska rhythm of your childhood

grandma cautions
be ready fah de unexpected
or it will mek yu blame yu own child
for coming when she come and yu
will lose out on the amity

this is the way you make a home

sit under a tree and negotiate with the stories inside your head

peel the yam and make sure its skin doesn't itch

take the pot from the stove   with your bare hands

caress your body and let your fingers spill pleasure   *grandma warns*
                                                when yu neighbours seh yu gwaan like yu
don't answer when someone calls your name in the dark   *betta dan dem*
                                                tell dem yu betta fah respecting dem
duppies know every crevice of a nice home   *an sharing yu yard's bounty*
and will strive to evict you   *wid dem but neva invite dem over*

don't sleep in your bed on the night of the full moon

home will *trace yu* up the cotton tree
from where you must retrieve your totem

leaving

when i had to leave home
tears wound down my cheeks
snot clogged my nostrils
and my chest was a hammered box
where wasps built their hives

                    my mother taught me to read tea leaves
                        this morning my grandmother

blue lights guided the ballad
                                appears in my teacup
to course over and through me
                                    sitting on a donkey
and when his body pressed into mine
                    when she sees that i recognise her
not even air could escape the scent   she presses her thighs into the side of the donkey
of home devoured by jealousy
                                  and shouts *giddy up*
                      her words are conveyed on the breeze
migration hoofed down the door
                      mark me word yu go haffi leave home
and home floated away
                                    soona or lata

the moon is kissed by the scent of home

lurid

behind the belly button
where you've tucked home
to escape the crass talk
and wild-flying fists

you clutch the sacredness of home
between your toes

don't tarnish this space
don't crumple these interactions

home is not a pointless compass

bright hopeful eyes have danced
through this space
if you listen carefully
you will still hear the giddy laughter
dusting home clean

grandma had a home
grandma left her home
grandma built her own home
grandma counselled
sequester home
in the dimple of your cheek

sneeze

the river stores the loss of the round house   in africa
where the man achoomed more than a dozen times
after his wife ran away from their home where love was a thief

a bright green house he had built   just for her   smoke made grandma sneeze
                                                                             but only if a fire was raging
achoom   one of her sons set the house
                                                                     on fire   wearily she commands
rumours incinerate what was once a cosy home   *never let your children know your home*
                                                                  is a reservoir   they will drink all the water
achoom

if …oom sounds
home will be swallowed by the river

where are we

did the house record their fighting

did they plant that baobab tree
rising from the dampness
vacuuming the mildew

what do you know about this home

sometimes the noise of home prompts escape

other times it is a labyrinth confused from
too many expectations

you cannot escape
the traps and claustrophobia of home

home is its own orbit that will never spit you out

grandma taps me on my shoulder
as i water the garden
she confides
*me go die at home in me own bed
when me ready*
one afternoon she went to lie down
and never rose

just right

the little girl refused to stop sucking her middle and index fingers
her mother rubbed pepper on them
her father smeared them with chicken poo
her grandma slapped and pulled them from her mouth
her grandpa threatened to chop them off

the little girl's behaviour muddied home

she was pinched for asking questions
ears twisted when she pushed back
elbowed in the side when she offered an opinion

grandma told me many practical
secrets

for some girls   home is padlocked

fi always have a good home
dash you pee across yu doorways

home was an anthill on an otherwise perfect lawn

garden fruit (egg-plant)

home is always a figment of what you hope you can achieve

in the earth's womb where the worms yawn for air
and the eggplants mauve as the lips
of some labia shout their firmness   you can take
solace in growing things

goats will show you how to survive even live on paper
and buck your way until home is no longer a mirage

i have come to realise
i must draw firm boundaries   even erect a moat
around my home if it is to be my haven

grandma instructs — fi protect yu
home mek garden fruit soup
only add scallion
den sit pan de
backsteps and drink de soup hot
money will prop up yu home

part ii

memories of home are
emotional wells
swathed in garlic

people and place collapse
in unreal time
unreal happenings
unreal realness

turning

in the house she shared with her mother and sister
her bed was pushed up against the wall
at nights the croaking lizards taunted her

having survived the dark days of the cocoon
the storyteller heard the abeng thundering   bouncing
from hill to valley to tree top to ocean waves

where their ancestors held their breaths   dove below
blue waters to gift a world too young to even crawl
the blueprint of crossing
a passage that didn't occur in the middle
this was the storyteller's most anthologised tale

she holds the enamel cup on her lap   filled with the
rich chocolate tea her grandmother made
grating cocoa and nutmeg   boiling coconut milk
mixing in molasses

home is buried in memory and nostalgia

turning 2

kneeling on her bed she gazed at the sunflowers
that grew outside by her window
some days their petals covered the floor of her room

pressed against the orange tree where her navel string had been buried
the storyteller showed them the sugar planted in their teeth
the ticks snaking through their blood
the distorted mirror where they would not recognise themselves
and the arrogant god who stomped on their ancestors

mother's love as enchanting as a bird of paradise
makes home a honeyed-safe place

turning 3

wrapping her arms around lilly's neck   she
was lifted from the bed and spoon-fed banana porridge

standing on the site where she was born the storyteller burped
the house in which she was born had been torn down but that did not mean
she had not been born there nor that her mother hadn't been ironing clothes
when her water-bag broke and when the cramps wound her back
she stomped her feet and clomped the iron on her husband's work shirt
burning out the pocket   the room singed in smoke
her mother tramping from one foot to the next and hollering
mercy mercy   let this child be born safe

home was the wet floor and a beige shirt with the
pocket burned out neatly folded in a drawer

the storyteller had witnessed flights and bodies somersaulting the stern

turning 4

each morning until she was four years old
she was bathed in a large basin and her feet rubbed with bay rum
her eyes followed the chicken pecking while her hair was plaited in three

the storyteller's voice was a pinhead that pricked the finger spewing blood
the sun turned on its side   as the wind flatus

the truth was in the word   she told them *birthed in spit and vexation*
the storyteller witnessed their fights and makeups
the man who was the father walking up to the woman who was the mother
as she was washing dishes wrapping his arms around her waist   pressing his body
into her   kissing her at the nape of the neck then laughter that made the
words a bold lie *don't think you getting off that easy*

the storyteller pushed her hands over her ears and turned away

to understand home   you have to use the machete to chop away the filters
and make-overs

turning 5

the neighbourhood boy   broke the wheel off her tricycle
and rammed the axle in her foot   pain too deep to cause blood

the storyteller learned fire was a balm when managed with love
but keep it away from home and your precious things
danger was fear nurtured in the heart
but fear was the house emptied   all the things tossed out

the storyteller saw what would happen and tried to forewarn them
don't imitate what you can never be or shouldn't even attempt to become
you will shed skin many times   becoming the becoming of uncertainty

the storyteller fanned herself and breathed deeply

every night before getting into bed she had to wash her feet
tap the mattress three times and kneel by the bedhead
and give thanks for all their lives

superstition and rituals safeguarded home

turning 6

doctor moody patted her head   bandaged her foot and enlightened
little boys often have to thrash around in blood until they learn to walk towards
friendship

the storyteller had the difficult task to disavow them
of the lie that they were descendants of ham
she tried with an analogy *the hand that grew food   prepared meals and*
 even sometimes clutched to another in desire if not love

they watched her as if she were mad
the storyteller braved their disbelief and fury
there is nothing more precious than yourselves and the ability to journey back
to home
to where some pieces of the puzzles no longer fit

the little girl was told *to be at home is to love yourself*
and the people who are family as steadfastly
as the blue mountains fling back hurricane winds

turning 7

she often kept company with birds
the yardman with his pronounced adam's apple
taught her how to whistle like various birds   frequently neglecting
to trim the edges which made her mother cross

they shut the storyteller away in the closet room devoid of colours
said she was delusional   they were giving her time to follow the rules
to stop being a heresy   creating chaos   the past was behind them
even if not forgiven
she was not their griot charged with their history   her stories were too heavy
calamity and misfortune   cliché   rubbish   move on
the storyteller bit her lips   pressed her hands to her mouth but still bauxite spilled
out

if you toe the line   home can be a sanctuary of protection

turning 8

she does not know if the story her mother kept telling of her
wild bravery   starchy as jackfruit pulp   was food for the future
or dust   subject to the nuisance of the wind   she suspected it was meant to serve
as a bridge but collapsed under the demand of truth

the storyteller broke her arm when she was four years old
when her father came insisting she was too far up and would fall
she fell   confirming her father's pronouncement that little girls should not climb trees
she did not want to sit with ankles crossed when she had ridden in the same hold
and survived the puking and shitting and smell of flesh slowly dying

the guavas remain untouched on the table   pungent as a slap in the face
the little girl did not eat them   too many seeds   and the storyteller dislikes them

any wonder home is rotting fruit

turning 9

as a girl she was not allowed to wander beyond the gate and amble
aimlessly as the boys
shirtless perspiration and disregard their kin   bravery stamped on their backs
but conformity was not a gene she was bequeathed   her tongue as loose as coins
in a pocket   challenged   interpreted and when that failed
she ran off feigning deafness

when they opened the door the storyteller's eyes were dry as flint and her voice
lacked contrition   bragging about being with nanny
being nanny   being a comrade

it wasn't even a full moon yet they knew madness was strange and unpredictable
the storyteller asked about zong and the maroon war and tacky war
they turned their backs and walked away but the storyteller kept listing this revolt
that uprising   that go-slow   scorching the fields to ash for their stoves

home is seldom a cup and saucer tea party
even when vigilant things get burned

turning 10

she beheaded the blond doll   cut off its hair   pulled out its arms and legs
then tossed the pieces between the hedge and the barbed wire fence
she wasn't interested in *playing house* or practising walking lady-like
instead she laid on her back and invited the sun to burnish her skin

the storyteller follows the moon orbiting the earth every 22.3 days
then she bolt-rushes around the sun   scattering stories as she sprints
a time before anansi when self was reflected in every tree in the forest
her scalp was anointed with liquid gold
bronze casting were done in every kingdom
here she goes again wid her long time saga like dat can free we they hissed

when home is messy the parables will ping on the floor like marbles
the little girl sits facing the wall   fingers in her mouth

knowing

the little girl was warned *don't swing upside down*
cover your cho-cho
don't walk through the short-cut alone
don't swim naked in the canal with the boys

never any dots to those lecherous men who slid their hands under
the elastic leg of panties   inserted their middle finger into the tender vaginas
of little girls

the storyteller knew a forgotten history had teeth and would eventually nip
she watched them watching her and the tale of admonishment grew
bubbles that popped but not iridescent

too much pain had been scrubbed into their bodies
too many dreams had been hacked from the roots
so living was the mantra
me jus waan live and nutten more   me surrenda to gad

the storyteller understood and shared their internment yet
she could not unhear the journey of the people who could fly   kinfolks
blood of her own blood   determination – her own will
fly   fly   fly   fly   fly   fly

the machination of home humbles the pyramids' architecture
causing the little girl to abscond home
sit under the breadfruit tree with her dog
until the swelling of her head shrinks

knowing 2

never afraid of the water the little girl swam early in the river and sea
catching jangas and paddling her feet to avoid jellyfish

the storyteller insisted on returning   returning haunted her
she carried the smell of home in the soiled sheets
she wound around her waist and x-crossed her chest   becoming a blue colour-wearing
pocomania devotee   she expected rain and flooding

the storyteller believed as long as salt sweated from the pores of her skin
there was hope   and while fruits on low hanging branches could blow down
those sheltered among the lush foliage at the top of the tree could endure

the little girl stood on the banking of the river on the opposite side of home
she could not merrily merrily row a boat to home
– her mother and father were drowning

knowing 3

when the little girl went to the bathroom
and found her panty soaked in blood
she returned to bed and decided to die silently
but only after stuffing the bloodied panty
in the dirty clothes basket and putting on a clean one
she was almost ten and only her paternal grandfather had died
and she remembered him packed with ice in the house with all of them
she hoped they didn't pack her with ice

the storyteller really tried   she scrubbed her tongue with carbolic soap
then hung it on the clothes line descending into silences
but the tales swirled as a dancing dervish

she wanted to tell them she understood the shame
they were not discarded shirts used to scrub grimy walls
and in due time she hoped they would rise sturdy and sure as bamboo
sometimes see and blind   hear and deaf is de only way
the market women advised her

the little girl woke to her mother's singing   she knew it was saturday
as her mother's baking wafted through the room   propped on her elbow
she looked across to her sister's bed and it was empty   *was she dead too*

it's almost impossible to not chew on cane dripping with sugar left at your door
the sweetness of home attracts bees and the deep desire to keep living

knowing 4

the little girl wanted to stay *little*   she wanted to continue playing
cowboy and thief with the boys   she wanted to lay hidden in the uncut grass
and glide with the clouds   she wasn't ready to be a woman yet

the storyteller stood in their path   ranting about justice as if that word
was yam or even a little piece of salt fish to season their rice
they didn't have time for her slave dirges   they had leapt across that river
had no intention of going back there
so they barbed-wire the storyteller's lips

whether oonuh pay attention or not de landscape tells a story of our continuity
she puttered
they ignored her
me know oonuh kyaan hear more than oonuh willing fi accept

the best place to keep the secrets of home
is rolled in your socks
you can always wash away the blood

knowing 5

the little girl was told *if you play with boys you'll have a baby*
a hamper load of anxieties engulfed her   she took refuge
in the closet   head brushed by the clothes   eyes blinded

before the storyteller could speak she was apprenticed to the griot
who instructed her in the language of transmission revealing multiple ways
to speak and be heard   but in every story were waves of pain with no ending

this is a story for girls the storyteller began   her thighs pressed together

in every part of the world one time or another
women's mouths   vaginas   ears
were cut and stitched   cut and stitched
cut and stitched   cut and stitched
cut and stitched   cut and stitched
cut and stitched   cut and stitched

on-and-on she droned   stuck and struck by the horror

cut
cut

stitched
stitched
cut
stitched
cut
stitched
stitched

stitched a caterwaul

home the little girl realised was blood and death   and no more playing

knowing 6

the little girl observed the pigeon flutter down on to the windowsill
she watched as it extended its head through the open window
and looked around before pecking at the seeds left there

shoo   screamed the girl   hands flailing
shoo   it's a trap   they will catch you
they say i'm a girl so stay inside and play with dolls
the girl shooed the pigeon and smiled as it flew away

when choosing to speak beware   you might become a renegade
the griot warned the storyteller
she knew this to be a truism but was unwavering
someone needs my story
the woman pushed up against the wall by the store owner
the helper whose employer's husband humped her
when she was scrubbing the bathroom

you will never find freedom at home
the little girl nodded her head and practised growing her wings

knowing 7

the little girl refused to continue piano lesson the piano teacher used his cane to tap
her fingers whenever she played a wrong note   she didn't care that all *nice* girls
knew
how to play the piano and do needle point   she didn't want to be a nice girl

thankful not to be stoned but   banished from the community
the storyteller rambled down the road   barefoot
her only clothes on her back
her head was a hamper full of stories

the road leading from home was zigzagged
carcasses lined the street
her life was the story of what happened to a woman who *gwaan* like man
back in those times which everyone wanted to pretend was a long time
enslaved women were hanged just like the men
and their babies cut from their swing bodies

the little girl remembered her grandfathers' ni-night
white rum poured in libation ingested by the older men
held in the mouth then sprayed in all the four directions
the rum would drive the duppies from home

often home needs a liquid spirit of protection
just like women

knowing 8

her sanctuary was the private burial ground   four raised and tiled tombs
even in the heat of the day they were cool and it was there the little girl took refugee
and began to write poems and stories that spilled from the storyteller's pockets

the storyteller's feet knew which path to take and which ones to avoid
weary but not defeated she slowed her breathing   listened
she heard the story jogging towards her   all trees have roots
she stopped by a dead stump and eased her body to the ground

thus began the storyteller's first story after being exiled
it was her own life she was seeing at another time
a time before now   when she was her ownself   sovereign

home is period cramps snaking up your thighs
but you continue walking until you are beyond the gate

knowing 9

whenever the little girl shared what she saw in her mind's eyes
she was accused of lying   she didn't abandon the wonders of her mind
she just stopped sharing

the storyteller surrendered to the asking of her body bent on its own destiny
she paused   her eyes being drawn to the bend in the road
anansi the old woman flagged her down
lamentation had formed a small pool around the woman's feet
her mouth opened but her hands spoke

*mi grandson   mi namesake ave run amock
mek everybodi believe him is me   dat me is not meself
dat me neva was him him was always me but me was me before him
dem catch me and him mama me dawta by de river a wash
dem chain we pan de boat him bawn in de hold
him mama me dawta screamin until her breath stop
me heart tun stale dumplin hard and dry*

*so me gi him me name   me teach him fi small up himself
me show him how fi build him own house
before dem push me overboard me push mi grandson
mi namesake unda a oman dress   tell her fi protect him
mek him grow strong   and him grow strong
me neva tell him tun jinal   but survival change de best a we
and anansi jus a survive   but now him need guidance
fi walk a different walk*

old woman anansi fanned the storyteller
that story was not done yet
the stories had no ending

you could grow strong at home if you know when to small up yourself
 and find the stories no one tells

knowing 10

the little girl thought about her father who came to visit
who took her to spend time with nanny   his mother
who taught her how to clean their parrot's cage

the storyteller smiled a knowing smile
she enjoyed telling the girl about the man who would become her father
before he knew her mother or that he would father her

the storyteller breathed deeply and so the story unravelled

one day for no reason that anyone   including the man could figure
the man walked to his field   but instead of ploughing or planting
he sat in the middle of the field and screamed at the top of his voice

his voice scared away the elephants for the entire day
he sat there bawling until his throat swelled and his voice was hoarse
yet he did not know why he was sad

when evening descended he decided it was time to leave
not just the field but the entire area
and go in search of what his heart was telling him

a house   a domicile   the place the little girl called home

knowing 11

the little girl cried when she saw the man who became her father
eyes red   heart shattered

the storyteller knows how to tell a stirring story

of the petite woman the man chose who became her mother
the same woman who almost lost her eyes   retinas taken out and scraped
for a week   her head placed between two cement bags   eyelids taped back
but the man would kiss her around the eyes and tell her they could see what he
would become   joined by a similar proclivity for life they rode their bicycles
from vineyard town to downtown and she watched him compete around race course
that would be renamed heroes circle
how the life they shared grew like the bananas and cane where they worked

even through the eye of a needle   the smiles that grow in a home
will thread the entire island

part iii

returning to return
she had to find the house
that was once home

but first she had to interrogate
what home means
and believe it existed
not just for her

she would have to relive
the experiences of home
to be home

sorting

the leaf you left hidden by the hollow trunk
has long been eaten by termites

but the breadfruit tree from which the fruit dropped
and killed your grandmother is much taller than you imagined
you stand under it daring a breadfruit to fall and bust open your head

all the footprints of your childhood have been washed away by rains
and breezed into other patterns you can't even read

the house is not liked you remembered it
everything is a myth warped into a time-freeze
nothing is as you recalled it

beware of tales the storyteller chants as facts

home is not what kills you

sorting 2

the little girl was told
her mother   her grandmother and she herself
were cut from the same cloth   – why cloth she wondered
what did three generation of women share in common
a tiny frame and ample posterior that warranted more attention
than they cared to navigate

returning home was being reminded that all men
– regardless of station – still felt privileged
to discuss her body whenever she entered
a public space

home is gritting yourself
for street sexual harassment

sorting 3

the explosion she heard was a round of shots.   a rocket of bullets
ringing through the evening   not festive or warning
gunning for someone who might or not make the news

before she can run safely home   the guilty and innocent bystander
lives will be clipped   how to survive beyond today
hopscotch   take cover   drop to the ground

as bodies salute the asphalt
the johncrows perched in trees hover
no need to outwait the prayers
no more running and dodging   bullets greet a body
bam   bam   bam   get ready for the undertaker

not even home is safe in this place
here a house never upgrades to become a home

sorting 4

when she was a girl   a rapist escaped   from spanish town prison
thought to be hiding out in the cane fields   awaiting women walking alone
the men of the community instructed
the women to walk in groups   keep girls locked inside

they the men did not go into the cane field and search for the rapist
almost all the homes were surrounded by cane field
they did not implement rotating guard for the community

being safe as a woman was a limbo contest

home was void of railing guards
just lip service and rapist on the loose

sorting 5

the body is both familiar and foreign   decent and indecent

that place between her legs was tabooed   yet her fingers played down there
wet   sticky   a swooning feeling   tasting herself on her lips

hands slapped   and washed   *don't let me ever see you doing that   nastiness*
seen and unseen things for which there is no language *just don't touch yourself*

vagina   the storyteller enunciates   *possessed by half the population   a noun*
vagina aka pum pum   honeypot   man's downfall

home paraded rules that made pleasure a sin

home 6

upon returning you are advised to call and get assistance from
the jamaica association for the resettlement of returning residents

i've lived in at least four houses before i left   can they all qualify as home
was each move a resettlement   if they no longer exist
does it mean i never lived in them   and what about my life there
are those events gone   demolished or transferred to the new occupants

– our second home at monymusk estate where daddy oversaw the
conversion of sugar into rum and caught barrels of crab with the other men
which mommy curried and made crab fitters

then mommy/sister/ me left daddy and we had our own tiny house
sharing one bedroom   a comma of a kitchen   a living room
a veranda that enclosed the house and a yard that was its own
island which i roamed with myriad of fruit trees on which i feasted
but that was only for a year until we moved into our real home and i
had my own bed again and the life of that house can fill realms

there is a certain magic in moving   but no one can remove me from
all the place where i've lived   i'm a migrant   i'm resettling

home 7

over many years, wide-ranging mechanisms have been implemented to guide
returning citizens through the resettlement process

there is no mechanism that addresses the constant noise
especially in rural areas nights are loud

a performance of crickets and other creatures
in kingston it's the sound systems blasting   bikes roaring and dogs yapping
on sundays the churches with their jesus praising and dirge songs
and even the house the storyteller was trying to make home
had its own sounds of family drama and silences that pinged

the storyteller tried to identify each sound
in returning she had vowed to decipher every detail
all the variegated tingles and hums of home

days of return 2

the language of return is written on parchment paper
its tale is old and banal   people are always returning
with things to safeguard them against what home lacks

the storyteller had books and art   no bed no fridge no sofa no stove
books   most of which she would give away   and art   most of
which she would keep and whatever else she needed she would purchase

the entrance to the door of return was wide open and when she paused
to take in the landscape it was a hibiscus promise and dutchie steaming
with mackerel run-down that erased all her longing for home

days of return 3

she built herself a round hut with thatched roof and bamboo poles
sealed with daub   no nails   my great grand aunt's house
where mommy deposited us every summer   for a week
to learn the value of life   she declared waving as she drove off
in her light blue anglia

aunt zilla who taught herself to read
from the newspaper she used to decorate the walls
she rejected toothpaste   said the ash from her coal stove
was better and when again i saw her at the age of 99 she still had
most of her teeth   her eyes still danced and she pulled
on my hand and said in disbelief   *is little cathy come back fah true*
she always said I was the spitting image of my mother

she had two children although no man was ever seen or known to visit
she was the village griot even though she only went to the river to wash

and when she died at 110   her hair plaited in two like she wore it from
a girl parted down the middle   the jackfruit tree withered and died the next
morning and a rolling calf was heard roaming that night

room and rooms of stories

every relative   the storyteller visits sings praises of her mother
how she sent money to buy bricks to finish the house
helped cousin nicey support jusminet to complete high school
pay for the hospital bill when diabetes took uncle emanuel's right foot

in the anglican church ledger she finds her mother's name listed as
godmother to almost thirty children over a sixteen-year span
and hears echoing in the creaking floorboards stained with bismarck
and shined with a coconut brush her paino rendition of johann strauss'
the blue danube waltz   that was when home stretched from caymanas
to flemstead village where everyone was related and the river rinsed
away secrets

now motherless and a returnee   with no fixed ties the storyteller
searches each room for its tale to stitch together a new home

days of return 4

home is a poem balanced on the hand of a clock

i was born close to midnight   easy and soft as green
lacatan banana boiled for breakfast

being the last child of that union   my father had long forgotten
his marital promises   slept out at least once weekly
returning home the morning after my arrival
my mother sheltered me from the fever of his rum breath

the hand of the clock moves but the poem is still unwritten

returning home   the storyteller decides these memories are zinc roof
leaking   warping the wooden floor that has been replaced with tiles
both mother and father are dead and she honours them for planting
her feet on this land and steering her home

scanning the landscape she knows not even death will conclude
this poem   home will always remain unfinished

days of return 5

as the storyteller sat in the back of the taxi the driver blurted *idiot*
it felt like a sharp jab in her side   she remembered the first time
the teacher said she was an idiot because she couldn't describe sleet
idiot that was the word they called us as slaves her mother had said
forbidding her to called anyone that

we were *idiot*   for running   *idiot*   for working slow
idiot   for refusing to submit   *idiot* for knowing when best
to reap the crops   *idiot* for setting the fields on fire

you eva see a damn idiot like that
the taxi driver turns in his seat seeking her agreement
she wanted to tell him stop   let's examine this word we
readily hurl at each other at the slightest provocation

look pan dat idiot woman driving   that dunce idiot pickney
what a idiot   how him could be such a idiot
stupid idiot   yu's idiot tekin yu time fi cross the road
dem damn idiot bike men   she look like a idiot

the storyteller took a deep breath
i've never seen a place with so many idiots
jamaica must be a country of idiots

idiot rolled like a ball wrecking home

days of return 6

morning she greets the elder   *a reflex from childhood*

respect   he intones   fisting his right hand raised in greeting

morning   *jah bless*   pedalling on his bicycle   he smiles into the morning

morning   *praises sister* she hums stepping around   feet moving swiftly

morning   *maanin maanin*   never singular   her face beams
her pace slackens   we lock eyes   pause   then continue on

morning   *mornin m'am*   said respectfully   solemn as
his pressed shirt

morning   *give thanks*   like a chant   that keeps him going

morning   *oh morning*   she says shyly   an afterthought   glancing over her shoulder

morning   maanin-maanin   *maanin lady* he replies   surprise written on his face in a
stained shirt and soles almost gone ambling

morning   face opens like an orange peeled and sliced in half
good morning my sister

my hearts gigs

morning and a good day to you too m'am

good morning

days of return 7

he is bouncing between rows of scallion   thyme and white yam
in the jostle and hustle of papine market his name is being called

he cups his hands and covers ears and keeps stepping avoiding the man
jogging to catch up with him   avoiding the vendors who are also shouting

blade yu nu hear de coal man a shout yu
but the man continues with long strides   his hands covering his ears
at last the pursuer catches up and inquires
yu no hear me a call an run afta yu from way back dere blade

blade turns briefly but keeps stepping
me ears tiad me kyaan hear yu today home a call me
blade heads towards the exit   leaving the pursuer scratching his head

amused the storyteller turns to a fellow shopper whom she does not know
this can only happen ah yaad   *a man like blade with tired ears*

days of return 8

thine feet should not tread upon the ground unshod
me is the slippers man   de guard and protector
of your feet   your sole is the pathway to your soul
that connects straight to jah   buy me slippers   wear me slippers
and tread yu way directly into the arms of jah

intrigued the storyteller invited the slippers man to her home
to wash and measure her feet   they sat on the veranda
she offered him a glass of coconut water   he brought
his own chipped white enamel basin in which he placed her feet
pouring a dash of rum   two pinch of salt and some bay leaves
then he cupped spring water from a clay jar into the basin until the
storyteller's feet were up to her ankles in water

slippers man massaged each toe intoning *jah blessing*
and the storyteller thought about that time long ago when
someone with large feet stomped mud tracks from the veranda
to the middle of the living room then stopped   that was the
slippers man   completing home's circle

part iv

strident voices
a consensus of concerns

a bullet only kills
death is death
belief in heaven and reincarnation
cannot assuage

but the swallowtail butterfly is not
extinct
it returns despite all odds

the scientists are dumbfounded
but not the storyteller

returning spaces

at an uptown cocktail party the storyteller is served stamp and go
yu mean frittass she blurts out loudly in the space where only *proper*
english is spoken everyone is university degreed
has vacationed in europe and their tongues trip them when they lament
tired of the wukless nega who don't seem to understand dat slavery
done and gone long time   if only dem would apply demselves

their home   children   yards   businesses are run and maintained by
wukless nega
their wealth   privilege and leisure are sustained by
wukless nega

is *wukless nega against whom uptowners measure themselves*
we are a true credit to our race   if only they would just apply demselves

the storyteller knows that those below cross roads are regarded as lepers

home has its classes   shame and scorn draw the boundaries

gardener turns landscaper

she didn't want the guinea grass in her yard
its tough stubbornness reminded her of black people's hair
a trait she had managed to perm away

while sceptical she allowed the gardener to use salt
sometimes folk wisdom can be held to light
but she would have none of it in her home
her helper had her own plate and cup and fork
in the pantry on the bottom shelf
cannot let these people believe they are as good as you

the storyteller listened and bit her tongue
the woman was after all her third cousin on her father's side
she could tell that the gardener   needing the work to feed
his children nodded but not necessarily in agreement
the storyteller watched the man work marvelled at his skills
before leaving her cousin's house she stopped to speak to him
you're more than a gardener   you're a landscaper
no small change in a title

not only rich people have home   the storyteller declared
the essence of home can be found among the flowers

a nameless return

dem sell me　　　*de damn wukliss people dem sell me out*
she insisted　　　from under the tarp at half way tree
from where she sold men shirts and underwear

her voice *sirened* as they shoved her in the police car
they said she grounded ackee seed then boiled it with oleander
invited him to her home then gave him the brew to drink from a china cup

serve him right　　she spat　　　*who tell him fi touch me girl child*

the storyteller knew this story　　　had in fact lived one aspect herself

she knew home was not always a safe haven for little girls
and mothers would have to reclaim their obeah to protect them

once returned

they found her body a week later in a ditch

the storyteller chants
before you run away from home   have another home where you can run

returning home was counting the numbers of women and girls
raped   mutilated   killed

returning again
(for kamau brathwaite)

Opal Palmer Adisa

he never wanted to leave   he was always returning
to keep our heritage from being devoured by bulldozers

returning despite the walls of resorts blocking him from writing
cordoning off the sea so he couldn't see them others returning
rising up and treading on the waves to shore

go back he whispered to the storyteller
return and others will return too

the cows mooed him home and the women
he saw rising from the land told him to stay despite the trials

go home he chants to the storyteller
return and we will all return

he will have returned when a volcano belches another island
where home belongs to all ah we

sorting 6

the little girl remembers being told frequently she was pretty
once while in trelawny an elderly woman hugged her to her sweaty bosom
then declared *what a handsome little gal   she handsome can't done*

thinking the woman didn't know the difference:
girls were pretty and boys handsome
the little girl pointed that out but the woman said
me glad yu have mouth fi go wid dat face cause yu go need it
as yu get older but just yu know a handsome oman
is both pretty and beautiful and me see dat in you

the storyteller didn't like telling this story that beauty was often a
vip ticket   especially for a man   he was allowed to be a stallion galloping to the win
in truth   features or skin colour or personality guaranteed ice cream on a cone or a
shared cup with siblings

the little girl grew to expect the living room treatment
an accomplished actress   she smiled demurely
sat with her ankles crossed and hid her dirty nails
a gregarious disposition paved a smooth road wherever she went

there is never equanimity at home when how one looks
is a measure for success

sorting 7

when the tam-cladded rasta man banged on her gate calling out *broom   broom*
the storyteller was surprised so little had changed   nostalgia gave him a sale

he nodded respect   raised his staff then studied her face
rub noni on de moles *on yr neck empress dat will stop de itchin*
and drink lemon grass fi breakfast and before yu go to sleep

his demeanor took the storyteller back to the fire and brimstone prophet
her grandma's rasta neighbour who like clockwork every friday clad in a white robe
with his red yellow and green belt   marched around his house condemning all those
in cahoots with babylon   it was his story of redemption that set the storyteller on
her path to pile the stories in a bankra   roll her catta and carry them on her head

home was sweeping the yard clean with a natural rasta broom so the stories could walk

sorting 8

returning   the little girl began to know her mother as the true land
that had been captured   was still owned
its nutrients sucked from its soil

the storyteller interrupted her reverie
let me tell yu a story dat will mek yu shake yu head

junior christie neva finish school but him nu wah bruk in people house
or holdup woman and grab dem purse so him pick wateva him can find
and sell fi feed himself   give a little change to him babymada now and den

him figure jamaica independent so no king no deh bout no more
(but is because him neva know queen still rule we from way a foreign)

well him spot de ackee   and since him no know why we would
have a governor general   and since we no have no king
den kinghouse mus belong to all jamaicans so him forward and pick

de woman magistrate dash him in jail fi 3 months fi 45 ackee pods
instead a gi him a job sweepin de road or even washin her car
is so our national dish get expensive justice

the storyteller brushes her palms together
and walks away   shaking her head
home still forbids the barefoot man from entering

sorting 9

the little girl had an affinity for real mad people
and mad people who weren't really mad
just misunderstood   just wanting someone to see them

she met him under the aqueduct   in the middle
of the sidewalk   asleep on cardboard
when she went for her 6 am walk

the storyteller interjects   points out to the little girl
that there was never an introduction to the man
who was either really mad or had just lost his way

one morning as the little girl   who is really a big woman
passed the man who was mad or otherwise
she heard in a worm's voice   *beg yu a bun*
his head slightly raised from his bed
returning she stopped at the gas station
purchased a bun and placed it beside him

he was sleeping or indisposed
thus began their understanding

once she saw him eating a pile
of mangoes fallen from the nearby tree
she ventured   *you should throw the skin and seed*
in the bush so bees don't bother you
the sidewalk was clean thereafter

whenever he saw her at half way tree or papine
holding his head erect   he said *beg yu a bun*

home is the place where you are heard
and you get a little of what you need

sorting 10

the little girl had a hideaway   above the closet
in the bedroom she shared with her sister
using the bedroom door as her ladder   she climbed on top
hiding behind the large stereo box packed with linen
faking her absence as she listened to the different conversations
the real and unrealness of them   the multiple stories

the storyteller grew weary when she told this story
she wanted the little girl to keep hiding
the streets were not safe   girls were kidnapped
raped   their bodies burned

home was a phantom the little girl would have to
keep redrawing

returning

when breasts first appeared as buds hard and sensitive
on the little girl's chest
her mother visited the storyteller to secure the special
protection story for girls
the story that would camouflage her daughter's stirring womanhood

the girl   curvaceous and affable   needed a vigilant story
to turn away the lecherous eyes of hungry men
and the wanton desire of uninhibited boys
to touch and degrade   because they
believed it was their right to defile prized things

the storyteller remembered that time in her own life
when mostly older men made her hate her flowering body
and even now she's startled by such forwardness

the little girl didn't know then the crime was not hers to own
but the storyteller whom she became instructed girls
how to use their tears to sharpen their weapons
how to use fear to grow muscles in their arms
and how to make their
voices thunder and name their abusers

home was sometimes not a safe place for girls
but it can be a space that helps them develop their voices

returning 2

there is no sense to be made of the killings   no logic to be detected

the storyteller kisses her teeth every time she has to tell this story
it makes her vex and her pores emit a sour smell like a baby's puke

the divide is on the same street those who live up the top
must not go to the bottom

two women were shot and killed on opposite ends of fourth street
two young women working and helping their mothers murdered

throughout the course of the day
two women under 20 were pitilessly gunned down

two women   two mothers' daughters
two young women   themselves mothers

the storyteller scours the newspaper and walks the street
pleading with people

do you know the two young women who were shot
tamara and shawna-kae   shawna-kae and tamara

did you see the gunmen   did you feel the bullets
women murdered   the many femicides

home is a war zone the storyteller must navigate

returning 3

you been gone too long   what you know

home cast you out as a foreigner when it doesn't want to hear you

she come wid her american ways   we just want to live like americans

the storyteller observes the woman sitting before her
using her outstretched hands she scans the woman's body

a returnee   at long last she has returned
she cannot find her way   she has no friends

nothing is familiar   no compass to navigate home

all her life she walked in her mother's fear   carted it around
held it in her lap and now even with death knocking

she doesn't know how to let it go

drop it and run   fling it away and wash your hands and be done

the lessons of home are ineradicable   stitched into your dress
boiled in the yam you are fed   become your unbecoming

returning 4

sometimes the storyteller met the face of cynicism
bony and hard like the head of a ram goat boiled into manish water

at such times she wished she could be more like the coconut tree
its head way above the ordinary

the storyteller was practising silence
silence was not agreement or was it
her stomach cramped   her ears rang
her fingers drummed   the voice of her conscience nudged

open your mouth and swallow   *just swallow*
being *home as*   *a returnee came with a price*
mistrust   *suspicion and talk of your alleged wealth*

the storyteller gathered the stories
*elderly **returning** resident shot dead*
*elderly **returnees** being violently targeted by criminals*
***returnees** face extreme **murder** risk*

the storyteller did not want the walls of home
to tumble down around her

returning 5

various provisions have been made to facilitate a seamless reintegration into the
jamaican society for our returning residents in several areas such as resettlement

the storyteller read the notice over and over — words shiving
easily through the strainer

various   an adjective in jamaica that means *it can go any way*
facilitate   a verb in jamaican lingo meaning *me will help if me can*
                                 but don't expect too much
seamless   *an adjective is wha dat mean again*
             ahho   man nu wear nu seam in dem pants no more

home is a linguistic pepper-pot
its meaning stirred in its own irie dictionary

returning 6

you had forgotten until you got back that dusk was the time of day
when   if you held your breath
you could hear the earth talking to the trees and insects

being home you heard all the sounds
including your daddy's insistence that made
you didn't want your daddy to be your daddy anymore

your 7th birthday party had ended   everyone had gone
your presents were piled on your bed awaiting your glee
this was your mother's house

her home where the fragrance of freshly baked bread
wafted through all the rooms every saturday afternoon
but here was your father insisting that he didn't have to leave

you wanted him to leave   leave quietly
so laughter didn't have to squeeze
under the door jam like a centipede

home was your mother standing by the open door
insisting that your father leave

returning 7

the storyteller was warned *watch what you say and do*
you are a returnee yu foreign justice *no always wuk here*

the rumour had arrived at her door more than once
but everyone washed their hands of it
the storyteller was determined to uncover the truth

face pressed against the window hands cupped to cover the glare
the storyteller blinked and retched knees buckled/heart in her mouth

she sees mister walters with a gun to jimmy's head
– his youngest son   the older having run off –
mister walters other hand is grasping jimmy's neck
pressed to his crotch his pants pooled at his feet

the storyteller's yanked the curtains pulling out the rod
i see him hurting that boy she screamed into the phone

the storyteller was carted off to an undisclosed location
even there she wasn't safe
her life could be snuffed for a shearer bill

some homes shelter abusive fathers
home was a sick father's incest going unreported
for far too long

returning 8

the storyteller handed her passport to the immigration officer
with an infectious smile   his face reflected boredom
how long yu staying   *i'm home*

this is not a Jamaican passport   *i am home   a returnee*
how long you staying   *i'm home railed from her lips*

his eye said poor fool   her smile began to crack
ah givin yu two weeks

***jamaicans who gave up their citizenship (and can provide proof of that
previous status) who wish to return home will be granted the status of a
returning resident   with the attendant benefits***

collecting her luggage the storyteller's lips tremble
she was a returnee indeed mother and father dead
could she be her own proof of citizenship

coming home didn't always translate into a welcoming home

returning 9

returning   the storyteller stepped into a river of memories

when she was a girl an aunt who arrived with a grip
wearing a pale-yellow dress with a bright pink slip underneath
that bled through the dress and which hung below the hem

the aunt took up residence in her sister's and her room
the unsmiling complaining aunt
who for months droned on about
unfair beatings she withstood as a child
food being taken from her mouth to give to your mother – her sister
on and on until their bedroom and the entire house
sounded like a troop of monkeys screeching
so that even after the aunt left and the mother vaporised the house
burning frankincense and myrrh to restore balance

thus the storyteller never accepts the invitation of relatives
over-staying could become a habit
home shelters the barrenness of that aunt
whose bitterness blaming surpassed cerasee

returning 10

the woman who sat on the aisle seat next to the storyteller
on the bus going to flemstead   was a returnee too
had left when she was not yet six   smelled of orange rind and twisted her fingers

when the bus took the curve sharply everyone
was thrust and leaned on one another   the woman's lips
brushed the storyteller's ears
mi going to the ocean to drown mi father

smiling the woman patted the wooden urn on her lap
the storyteller smelled her distraught
and saw defeat written all over her slumped body

her father had always planned to return as a big man with money
but all he left was a house in need of repair
but had made the woman – his oldest – promise to take his remains home

the storyteller did not say to the woman *there is no ocean in flemstead*
only a river   the storyteller suspected the woman could be a relative
forgotten as a result of migrating   she would take her to the river
patch up broken family lines and together
they would welcome the father home

home was scattering the ashes of the dead to tie him firmly to home

returning 11

it was the same dream   the storyteller kept dreaming
of the hurricane winds that blew down the light poles
trapping her sister and her outside the wind whooshing their clothes
the wind trumpeting their bodies like a possessed musician

they had returned to the childhood home of the storyteller
there was a piano on which she banged and an anger surged
recalling the music teacher who tapped hard on her knuckles
every time she played a wrong note regret now
she gave up piano lessons and will never be able to play
strauss's *the blue danube waltz* like her mother

so many desires abandoned

the storyteller didn't want any child to be hit

in the dream the sisters roped their hands around each other
and withstood the winds that transported them home

in the season of sorrel and drought
the sound of her mother playing the piano
was the home locked in memory the same as the home
being lived now

returning 12

every good wish on your return home

the welcome message got trapped in the storyteller's head
what was there to wish for at her age beyond safety and respect
neither of which her country could guarantee her

the news was neither good nor assuring about the fate of returnees
for many the island was still a basket with an unravelled bottom
bobbing in the sea

the storyteller chuckled at the whatsapp thread circulating

returnees need fi have dem head examine
dem gone too long fi know any betta
dem tink jamaica easy   dem think Jamaica is a nice place
dem think jamaica want dem old body fi suck up de sun
we only want dem foreign pension fi keep the budget goin
wha dem go do when dem get sick and need medicine
tek phensic   dem tink dem denture can manage
the cornmeal dumplin and yam of dem childhood
mek dem galang bout dem a come home   come home to wah
de gun man dem an if dem no buck up de gun man dem
dem owna wuklis no-good family will kill dem off
with de beggin so dem can inherit dem house

yes oonuh come back to sweet Jamaica dat is only in oonuh mind
return yes but mind yu don't choke on the fish and festival

home nu easy at all

returning 13

the storyteller knew that time was not fixed in stone
but some things she hoped were unaltered

for 50 years the naseberry sweetness
of their friendship comforted her through many winters

upon returning she reaches out to him   he invites her
to his home to meet his children   they are home but do not
come to greet her even after he calls them repeatedly

he hands her a glass of limeade   asks if she still loves it
she nods   they sit in awkward silence   he doesn't remember
them ever pricking fingers in his back yard or that she brought
the safety pin they used to prick the skin of their pinkies
mingled their blood and swore to be
brother and sister and best friends forever

noticing her distress he sputters
your house was the only safe place
your mother always made me feel at home

what is home if the memories are a lie

returning 14

your sister with whom you shared a room for seventeen years
will not remember the day your father was drunk and drove
his car into a ditch   you were sitting on his lap and he told you
to steer   you were five years old   men pulled you
both out and you wobbled home
your father's laughter a thump in your ear

when your father related to your mother what happened
she clutched you then ran her hands up and down your body
asking if anywhere hurt

turning to your father   you saw her face inflamed
she barked at him *mi can't trust you with mi children*
he slapped her hand

that night she slept beside you in your bed   not in their room

sometimes pain gets flushed down the toilet and
rum is thrown down the drain
other things get mislaid at home
vanishing in the spaces of forgetting

until you return home to that same ditch
and you *reiki* your body to finally
dislodge your fright

part v

You are born into a home
you grow into that home
and no matter how far you travel
how hard you try to disassociate
you will spend the rest of your life
reliving home
trying to wash it from your skin

but
for better or worse
home is etched into your pigment

days of return

I
everyone who leaves thinks about home
and plans to return at some point

memories of basket stacked with ackee
fields as parched as the devil's mouth

home looped through the storyteller's mind
home   a word of hunger and longing

some vow never to return
some want returning to be a special occasion
some plot their return

monday might be the best day to return
everyone at work and school
your arrival is secretive   no witness to feed the susu

tuesday evening just as night begins to fall
children are getting ready for bed
you slip in unnoticed

wednesday when the bread is almost gone
slip in while the helper is cleaning and pause
to relive your first kiss at thirteen
tongue in your mouth and you wondering
should you bite or suck or something else

maybe you should return on thursday during the cricket match
sit on the spectators' bench
shout and rise from your seat
when the batsman hits a six

friday   might be the best day
join the men going home after work

who stop to pick and wolf down mangoes
picking at the hairs trapped between teeth

no return gallantly on saturday
your return disrupting routines — going to the market
but if you time it just right you'll be rewarded with
a large bowl of chicken foot soup with pumpkin
yellow yam and pimento seeds bobbing
and when you bite into the scotch bonnet pepper
your pores will open like a faucet and sweat will caress you

return on sunday during church service
stand by the gate and await their return

home is where everything is familiar and you are known

II
you couldn't imagine that there might be another place
different from the place you knew as home
that would steal you away forever or for a long time
or for forever or even longer than forever
a similar home but not the home-home you knew and loved

for everyone who has left home and is thinking about returning
there is an anglican church at caymanas estate
with a ledger dating back more than fifty years
that captures your mother's commitment to godmother
many children who needed bread   exercise books
school uniforms   an educated person to speak to the principal
about how bright they are and regardless of class
should be directed towards the academic track
when home does not offer the possibility to become
more equal for all

sit piously in the back pew move your lips but don't join the singing
your voice will give you away   put a little something in the collection plate
but slip out before the procession to the back door
where the pastor will shake hands and inquire *so you have come home now*

remember
home is never loss even when you have not returned
when you cannot remember names or faces
or if that short cut from your house to the river
still exists or a new house now blocks what used to be
your very own path

homecoming

the storyteller does not leave any footprints   even on wet sand
no track leading to home

she walked until emptied of thought by the autonomous ocean
trust was the lesson   you cannot rely on your memory
you cannot trust home   she paused to read the sign

upon returning to jamaica ensure that the vehicle transporting
you from the airport is covered so as not to have luggage in plain sight

wouldn't it be better to come home empty-handed then
capture land in the hills   build a shack
steal electricity   buy an ugly black plastic water storage tank
dump your garbage in the bush   park your van anywhere and sell from the trunk

coming home is buying sugar cane and jerk by the side of the road
feeling the desperation as you get below devon house
making sure to avoid standpipe and only going downtown
as an excursion and preparing as if you are going into a war zone
you are entering into a war zone
and the people who live there
in those places are still forgotten   still discarded

they are a part of home too
they are home still trying to make home homely

home

the storyteller's fear grows like grass – gluttonous
taking back the path leading to the house no longer occupied

thinking she will break if she doesn't hold onto
the memories associated with this house
the family gathering when three generations
were all dressed in blue – not by design
or that other time that distant cousin found their house
and knocked after midnight having walked over 20 miles
or when her mother's favourite bowl slipped from her hands
shattered into shards and she declared
death was coming on the wings of a mosquito

in the space of two weeks   an aunt a cousin and a grandnephew died
none previously ill

the storyteller hopped from one foot to the next
keep/sell/sell/keep this green and beige painted house
with its veranda crowded with ferns philodendron
african violets   dumb cane rubber tree and
myriad gatherings this is what she sees
not the cracked tiles or water eroded window frames

home despite all its warped memories
will always be more than a house   keep home

home 2

your mother raised pigeons that your bengali neighbour
sometimes caught and curried and then sent a bowl for your family
which your mother promptly tossed in the garbage

everyone wondered about the whereabouts of his wife
or why his fifteen-year-old daughter slept in his bedroom
when there were two bedrooms

sometimes you stood in the corner and peeped through the window
your stomach cramping as you watched the neighbour naked
pressed against the back of the chair where his daughter sat
pretending to read

home was a telescope into unspoken things like child abuse and incest
adults whispered disapproval   but never intervened

now you have returned and there are many girls like that girl of your childhood
in neat-starched uniforms who daily try to fend off fathers and uncles and cousins and
mothers' boyfriends and strangers   who rake their bodies and maim their minds as

they sit at home pretending to read   praying that home was a haven

home 3
(for mervyn morris)

sometimes the only thing to say about returning is
there is no need to explain yourself
everywhere you look has a familiar history

you go back to that day the government chopped down the oldest cotton tree
near the ferry police station and a host of people gathered
to witness   to protest   to lament

your mother said progress often leads to bereavement
you remember her placing the limb of the cotton tree
she had taken that faithful day in the garden where she grew vegetables

every time you drive on mandela highway   just below the ferry police station
you see that cotton tree and you wish everyone could see it too
and know you are home

returning is placing markers to indicate what has been uprooted
what is lost to gain what we have gained
the trajectory of home gets deleted from the history books

home 4

*we see your choice to resettle as a vote of confidence in the
jamaica constabulary force's ability to deliver quality service
that makes you feel safe*

you read the brochure and burst out laughing you can't control your hysteria
you say to yourself they must think because you're a returnee
you're stupid that you don't listen to the news
about police being shot at regularly or you don't cringe
every time you pass one of those zoso checkpoints with soldier boys
with machine guns who are often from places they are running to escape
and therefore will shoot despite their training
that has to compete with what they have lived all their life

your hysteria blinds you with tears
you grieve as you reflect on terms such as

      vote of confidence
      ability to deliver
      quality service
      feel safe

you are laughing so hard your entire body hurts
you get a hold of yourself and ponder
since returning almost everyone you have talked with
has very little confidence in the ability of any entity
to deliver quality service to anyone   let alone returnees

no one feels safe in jamaica despite the numerous security guards
gated communities   car alarms and grilled windows and doors

if you get sick you will be advised to fly off the island

home is not safe for most   home will not keep you healthy

home 5

i can always swim home   swim to what is expected
swim to what is troubling   swim to what is never spoken but understood

that day you and your sister were home alone
you both spotted mister cole approaching the gate
(the community elder who made our skins crawl)

you both hid under the mahogany table
so you didn't have to greet him or open the door
you clinched hands tightly imagining waves taking you
out to sea bobbing like logs seaweed snagging our feet

you treaded water until the sun dove into the sea
and mommy came home
then all the salt water spilled from your mouths

mister cole swallowed by the waves
and you and your sister didn't drown

returning home you read about children drowning
some by their pastors   – two sisters
(not unlike you and your sister who escaped)
raped   impregnated
yet expelled by the community that
is more concerned about protecting
the church's reputation than their children

you wonder about this home
where the sea can never rinse away the children's fear

days of return 8

sitting on the curb lamenting his plight to himself
is a poor man evidence from his scruffy
shoes and clothes he gesticulates in a raised tone
self-flaggellatory
me pick a bag a ackee and tek dem to market fi sell
it cost me $200 fi go there me sell all the ackee fi $400
it cost me $200 fi get back home   weh de profit in dat
why ackee suh badminded and wukliss

bad words hopped from his mouth like rabbits

on a rainy thursday morning a few weeks later about 6 am
the storyteller sees the same man standing in the middle of mona road
using a stick that's much too short to pick ackees
frustrated at not being able to knock any down
he turns out all his pockets   a lone ackee falls to the ground
bending he picks it up   rubs it on his pants then bites into it
head back in supplication he beseeches

de lawd is fi me shephard
him mek me tred on dis mona road safe
him lead me from the wrath of august town
wid all de shooting an killin
me is me own comfort
me no fraid fi not one of dem jinal politicians
fi me rag an stick will always be wid i
one a dem days me will have a big table
spread wid plenty sweet food
for goodness an mercy must follow i
all de days of me miserable life
for me a go dwell in jah house
faheva and eva
ahman

home is this man — one among many
trying to survive against all odds

queen *kumina

i am she who heals   dancing until my perspiration divines
who needs a laying on of hands   or to trash about on the ground
twirling until the fever runs away   or who needs rum spewed
into the face in order to see the worth of her own hands
or who needs a hand on their abdomen to open the womb
who needs an anointment to incise the arthritic knee
who needs a hex to drive away the husband whose fists are bombs

i am she who heals   pour libation in four directions
let the sound of the drums ascend beyond the clouds then sink
below the navel of the earth
let the voices chant slicing the night open
let feet shuffle in apology for hesitating too long
and let those who have belittled themselves hear me coming in
the wind and catch the spirit of my resistance in the swirl of my dress
in the beads of sweat clinging on my brow
and laugh into the dance of liberation

i am she who heals   my heart ignites the dawn
dance with me   dance and let our feet name
this place memory   ancestry   freedom

home

*Kumina is a healing ceremony in Jamaica that has its roots in the Congo, Central
Africa, and is also linked to Myalism. It involves drumming, dancing, spirit possession,
ritual sacrifice and herbalism. Some conflate Pocomania and Revivalism with Kumina.
Research suggests that Kumina might be derived from a few Ki-Kongo words, such as
Kumina, and Kumu, which means to move in a rhythmical manner, and to mount up,
respectively.

key-man lock de door and gone*

key-man has locked another door
issuing a plaintive call-and-response
from the community

key-man key-man they lament and the leader confirms
key-man lock de door and gone

no room to bargain   the mirror held to the nose
not a smear   mirrors are covered with white lace
her shoes put by the front steps

key-man death's executioner   came in the middle of the night
just as she got into bed   he locked her door

and all the wailing of his name bitter as cerasee on their tongues
will not breathe back life   but still they chant
key-man key-man the drummer counters
key-man lock de door and gone

they move cautiously   aware sooner than later their door will be locked

they cannot oppose him   ready or not
when he puts the key into the lock   only the living will sing you good bye
but really they sing to key-man   hoping their dirge might keep him
away from them for another day   another year   a little more time

feet stomp into the ground
the middle of their palms connect in a harsh clap
they hold each other around the waist and
twirl and bump   their voices forever constant   bewailing
key-man key-man pleading *don't come around here anymore*

the drum knows the truth and sends the message
loud and clear into the air leaving
no doubt   key-man done *lock de door and gone*

*Jamaican folk song in the Revivalist tradition and sometime included in the Ni-Night
(Nine Nights) celebration, held to celebrate the dead and cheer up the bereaved,
through suggestive dancing and music.

ancestors

when we learn the name of the nameless   we will not be nameless

the storyteller is soaking in a metal tub under the tamarind tree
lavender   basil and lemon grass perfume the water
she uses the loofah sponge to scrub and song her body

when we own what we know   our knowledge cannot become unknown

the birds are watching the storyteller bathing outside in the evening air
they gather on the tree branch chirping their assent   but warning
mind yu catch cold   yu nuh so young anymore yu know

before all that we have gets erased   register your deeds
sweeten your yarns with condensed milk and feed it to your children
disavow modesty be purposeful   consistent   unwavering

the storyteller uses the calabash to pour water on her head
she closes her eyes   uses one hand to wipe the leaves that linger on her face
mother owl watching   click-clicks her tongue   *she sure fi get cold now*

thinking she sees someone the storyteller calls out
is duppy or living being   no response
she giggles but is not done   *me catch yu*

the storyteller nibbles on jerk coconut-flakes   sips lemon grass and mint tea
allows the rhythm of the drums to transport her   surging through her body

every story has a ni-night and every *gone-home* happens in a yard
the storyteller stands up in the tub and kuminas home

sankofa

run go home

    how do i return when i never left   even after getting on the plane at palisadoes
    even after looking down after the land disappeared   even after my heart crumbled
    and i wailed inside   i was always   there   home   covered over with dry banana
    leaves brownie my dog sleeping at my feet   the turquoise ground lizards crawling
    close by my leg

hurry home

    inside was harmony   everything had a place   the staging of the books in
    the mahogany bookcase the starched crochet dollies on the centre table
    even how she wrapped her school books   the dresses in the closet
    church dresses going out dresses school uniforms   hats in boxes
    on the shelf on top   shoes   lined in a row same order as dresses but
    mostly there was love   hugs and kisses   always food and music
    mother playing the piano or 45 spinning on the stereo fats domino
    singing   the house sang itself into a safe space

home ah call yu

    weh yu been   how yu walk about suh   yu been gone so long
    yu face almost leave me eye   is true yu come back fi true
    dis lang time gal me neva see yu no place like yard
    de mackerel run down with roasted yam   yard sweet cyaan done

    having returned the storyteller listens to the kaskas and moves through the hustle
    sometimes she retreats into her hammock and only listens to the birds
    whose stories she is yet to tell
    chewing on a piece of cane she wipes the juice that's trickling
    down her chin with the back of her hand
    and laughs her mother's laugh

    lawd lawd   lawd   me nu waah dead yet
    but me will die here   home at last
    sankofa

returning to return

every time you leave and return   you have to invent another story

the storyteller hummed in a soliloquy   she knew the listeners
of her stories came for healing and guidance
or simply because they had nowhere else to go and although
doctors sometimes prescribed pills   that did not quiet the chatter
of the audience conversing inside their heads

every story has an owner   the storyteller belched

some homes require silence   the silence of a doorknob
the silence of the house
before it was ever occupied   before someone turned it into a home

the little girl crawled into the hammock with the storyteller
that was slung under the ackee tree
they were wrapped in the covid pandemic
and contemplating the meaning of home
and returning to return   have they returned
or were they still returning   trying to return to what was no longer
what were warped memories
what was a longing for what really never was

having at last returned the little girl retrieved that part
of herself that she had been missing
for so many years

the storyteller sequestered the little girl's returning
kneaded it into a dumpling
then flung it into the sky   a rainbow for all returnees' returning

wheel and come again
                    me deh home!

About the Author

Opal Palmer Adisa uses language to shapeshift and call other realities into being; a cultural activist, gender specialist, and an award winning writer of over 20 books in all genres, Adisa is the former University Director of The Institute for Gender and Development Studies- RCO at The University of the West Indies, Mona, and Professor Emerita of California College of the Arts, Oakland, California. She is also a playwright and director whose plays have been produced in California, St Croix & St Thomas, USVI, and Egypt. Further, she has been awarded artist-in-resident at several prestigious venues, including Sacatar in Brazil, El Gouna in Egypt, and McColl Center for Art and Innovation in North Carolina, and Headlands Center for the Arts, California.

Publications:

Portia Dreams, the authorized children's biography of Portia Simpson Miller, Jamaica's first female Prime Minister, Poretian Simpson Foundation, 2021

Dance Quadrille, Play Quelbe, children's. Pulmeria, 2018

Love's Promise, stories, CaribbeanReads, 2017

Look! A Moko Jumbie, children's, Plumeria, 2016

4-Headed Woman, poetry, Tia Chucha Press, 2013

Incantations & Rites (with devorah major) poetry, The Literary Leaf/ Deconstructed Artichoke Press, 2013

Painting Away Regrets, novel, Peepal Tree Press, 2011

What a Woman Is, poetry with paintings by Shyam Kamel, 2010

Amour Verdinia, poetry, chapbook, The Literary Leaf/Deconstructed Artichoke Press, 2009

Conscious Living, poem, chapbook, The Literary Leaf/Deconstructed Artichoke Press, 2009

I Name Me Name, poetry/essays , Peepal Tree Press, 2008

Playing Is Our Work, children's, WWWAC Press, 2008

Until Judgment Comes, short stories, Peepal Tree Press, 2006

Eros Muse, poetry/essays, Africa World Press, 2006

Caribbean Passion, poetry, Peepal Tree Press, 2004

The Tongue Is a Drum (poetry/jazz CD with Devorah major), 2002

Leaf-of-Life, poetry, Jukebox Press, 2000

It Begins With Tears, novel, Heinemann, 1997

Tamarind and Mango Women, poetry, Sister Vision Press, 1992

Fierce Love (poetry/jazz recording with devorah major),1992

Traveling Women (poems with devorah major), Jukebox Press, 1989

Bake-Face and Other Guava Stories, short stories, Kelsey Street Press, 1986 & Flamingo, 1989

Pina, The Many-Eyed Fruit, children, Julian Richards Associates Publisher, 1985

Editor:

100+ Voices for Miss Lou: poetry, tributes, interviews & essays, an anthology, The UWI Press, 2021

Caribbean Erotic, poetry, prose, essays – an anthology (co-edited with Donna Aza Weir-Soley), Peepal Tree Press, 2010

Interviewing the Caribbean: Caribbean Music, part 1, An online/print journal, 196 pages, Spring 2021

Interviewing the Caribbean: Kamau Brathwaite, part 2, An online/print journal, 154 pages, Spring 2020

Interviewing the Caribbean:, Kamau Brathwaite, part 1," An online/print journal, 134 pages, Fall 2020

Interviewing the Caribbean: Caribbean Childhood: Traumas + Triumphs, part 2," An online/print journal, 164 pages, Spring 2020

Interviewing the Caribbean: Caribbean Childhood: Traumas + Triumphs, part 1," An online/print journal, 156 pages, Spring 2019

Interviewing the Caribbean: Caribbean Femininity + Masculinity = Gender Justice, part 2, An online/print journal, 156 pages, Spring 2019

Interviewing the Caribbean: Caribbean Femininity + Masculinity = Gender Justice, Volume 4 part 1," An online/print journal, 156 pages, Spring 2018

Interviewing the Caribbean: Caribbean Life + Olympian Feats, part 2 An online/print journal, 156 pages, Spring 2018

Interviewing the Caribbean: Tribute to Derek Walcott, An online/print journal, 156 pages, Spring 2017

Interviewing the Caribbean: Caribbean Life + Olympian Feats, part 1 An online/print journal, 156 pages, Winter 2017

Interviewing the Caribbean: Violence in the Caribbean, part 2 An online/print journal, 169 pages, Spring 2017

Interviewing the Caribbean: Violence in the Caribbean, part 2, An online/print journal, 169 pages, Fall 2016

Interviewing the Caribbean: Intellectual Property, An online/print journal, 169 pages, Fall 2015

ProudFlesh, Riding The Waves of Caribbean Women: poetry, prose, essays an art, 220 pages, Issue 8, 2013.

The Caribbean Writer: Ayiti/Haiti, Volume 25, journal of poetry, prose, personal narrative, interview and book reviews; translated into French 640 pages, 2011.

The Caribbean Writer, Volume 24, journal of poetry, prose and essays, 420 pages, 2010.

Adisa's children's poem have been anthologies in many collections.

Adisa's essays on gender and other women's issue is available in several anthologies.

**look out for my next
poeticprose collection
entitled,**
*my body in the land of
xaymaca,* forthcoming 2023